Published in the United States of America by
Cherry Lake Publishing
Ann Arbor, Michigan
www.cherrylakepublishing.com

Content Adviser: Dr. Todd Kelley, Associate Professor of Engineering/Technology Teacher Education, Purdue Polytechnic Institute, West Lafayette, Indiana
Reading Adviser: Marla Conn MS, Ed., Literacy specialist, Read-Ability, Inc.

Photo Credits: © Paolo Costa/Shutterstock Images, cover; © Sevda Stancheva/Shutterstock Images, 4; © Lissandra Melo/ Shutterstock Images, 6; © hans engbers/Shutterstock Images, 8; © Massimiliano Pieraccini/Shutterstock Images, 10; © Jim Guy/ Shutterstock Images, 12; © Eduardo Estellez/Shutterstock Images, 14; © superjoseph/Shutterstock Images, 16; © Albert Pego/ Shutterstock Images, 18

Library of Congress Cataloging-in-Publication Data
Names: Loh-Hagan, Virginia, author.
Title: Bridges / by Virginia Loh-Hagan.
Description: Ann Arbor : Cherry Lake Publishing, [2017] | Series: 21st century junior library. Extraordinary engineering |
    Audience: K to grade 3. | Includes bibliographical references and index.
Identifiers: LCCN 2016032400| ISBN 9781634721622 (hardcover) | ISBN 9781634722940 (pbk.) |
    ISBN 9781634722285 (pdf) | ISBN 9781634723602 (ebook)
Subjects: LCSH: Bridges—Juvenile literature. | Bridges—Design and construction—Juvenile literature.
Classification: LCC TG148 .L64 2017 | DDC 624.2—dc23
LC record available at https://lccn.loc.gov/2016032400

Cherry Lake Publishing would like to acknowledge the work of The Partnership for 21st Century Learning.
Please visit www.p21.org for more information.

Printed in the United States of America
Corporate Graphics

CONTENTS

Fallen trees are nature's bridges.

What Are Bridges?

Bridges let people travel over water and gaps. Careful planning goes into building bridges. Engineers study how bridges work. They make bridges safe. They consider **spans**, or distances. They consider weight. This is **load**. Load depends on what crosses the bridges.

Forces push. Forces pull on bridges. Engineers balance these forces. They make bridges stay in place.

Bridges must be able to support heavy loads, like trains.

Bridge **decks** need support. They carry heavy loads. Load causes forces to press down and stretch out. Too much force in one area can cause bridges to fall down. Engineers design bridges to move forces from weak to strong spots. Engineers use **beams**, **arches**, **trusses**, and **suspension** designs to move forces.

Look!

Find a bridge in your town. Look at it. What type of bridge is it? What does it cross? How long is it?

Beam bridges can be 250 feet (76 meters) long.

How Are Short and Long Bridges Supported?

Beam bridges cover short spans. Two **piers** are on both sides. Beams are placed over the piers. Weight pushes down on the beams. Forces bend in the top. Forces bend out the bottom. Too much force breaks the beams.

Making beams longer doesn't help. This is unsafe. But engineers can make beams thicker or use more piers. This makes beam bridges stronger.

Trusses make a pattern on the Jacques Cartier Bridge in Canada.

Bridges using long beams are weak. But short beam bridges can be linked. Engineers connect them together to cover long spans.

Long bridges need trusses, or supports made of triangles. Triangles spread out forces to strong parts of the bridge. Trusses are placed above or below bridge decks to take load away from decks.

Ask Questions!

Ask friends how they feel about bridges. Some people are scared. They don't like crossing bridges. Why are bridges scary to them? How do they avoid bridges?

Arches can't be too wide. Wide arches are weak.

How Do Arch Bridges Work?

Force totally supports arch bridges. An arch connects two **columns**. Decks rest on arches. Load pushes arches together. This tightens stones. Stones move together. Stones have slanted sides. Arches push down on stones' sides and down to the ground. Forces are carried along the sides. They go to columns. Columns push back on arches from the ground. This keeps arches from spreading apart.

Ancient Romans made stone arch bridges like the
Alcántara Bridge in Spain.

Some arch bridges have **keystones**. A keystone is the top middle stone of the arch. Load rests on the keystone. It moves down the other stones' sides. Solid rock **anchors** arch bridges. The rock pushes against arches. This makes bridges stronger.

Engineers can put many arches together to make long bridges. These bridges are strong. But they take a lot of time to build.

Think!

Think about Newton's Third Law of Motion. It states that for every action, there is an equal and opposite reaction. How does this apply to bridges? Why is it important?

Suspension bridges, like the Golden Gate Bridge in California, can span over 7,000 feet (2,134 m).

How Do Bridges Hang in the Air?

Suspension bridges use **cables** and towers. This is how they balance forces. Cables are anchored on each side. They're strung over the towers. They slope down and back up. **Suspenders** attach decks to cables. They hold decks in place. Towers support the weight. They spread out forces. Forces move from cables to the ground.

Cables create arcs, or curves, between towers on the
Lions Gate Bridge in Canada.

These bridges have a cable support system. Cables move forces around. Anchors pull outward. They pull on the towers. They pull with the same force as decks. This balances weight.

Wind creates forces. It makes bridges sway. This is a problem. It's unsafe. Engineers design trusses underneath. Trusses keep bridges steady.

Try This!

Materials

2 books that are the same size, 2 stacks of books that are the same size, string

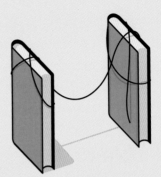

Procedures

1 Stand two books up, facing each other. Place them about a foot (30 centimeters) apart.

2 Tie string around the top of one book. Let the string hang loose. Tie the other end to the top of the other book.

3 Apply force and press down on the center of the string. This will cause the books to fall. This is what engineers want to avoid.

4 Stand the two books up again. Put the stacks of books on the outer faces of each book. Create a span between the standing books.

5 Hang a string over the tops of the standing books. Put the ends of the string under the stacks of books on both sides.